Original Story and Character
By: Roshika West

Learn About: Creativity, Family and Never Giving up!

The Little Artist

Original Story and Character

By: Roshika West

Copyrights:

Copyright © 2023 Roshika West
All rights reserved.

No part of this publication may be reproduced, distributed, or transmitted in any form or by any means, including photocopying, recording, or other electronic or mechanical methods, without the prior written permission of the publisher, except as permitted by U.S. copyright law.
For permission requests, contact: www.learnmediapublishing.com.

The story, all names, characters, and incidents portrayed in this production are considered fiction. No identification with actual persons (living or deceased), places, buildings, and products is intended or should be inferred.

Written By: Roshika West
Illustrations by: Roshika West and Hameo Pham
Book Design By: Roshika West

Publisher: Roshika West
20-West Ent. & Media Co. LLC.
Publishing Division: Learn Media Publishing
Direct Contact: www.LearnMediaPublishing.com

Text and Illustration Copyrights © 2023 Roshika West

Art By: Roshika West

Dedication:

"Tell your story," my great-grandmother said.
And tell my story, I did.

So I wrote this book to tell my art story and lessons
growing up. It is a true story about life, learning,
creativity and family. This book is therefore
dedicated to my great-grandmothers and
grandmothers.

I thank them for everything, especially the gift of
creative expression.

Original Story and Character

By: Roshika West

Hi, I am Sunny and I like to draw! Here's how it all started....

On one Bright and Sunny day, I took a walk. First, I saw circles and shapes around my room. Then I saw circles on my jacket and in my cartoons.

I noticed, everywhere I look
there are shapes and colors: like
Greens, Purple, and Blues—I
even noticed the Pink on my new
shoes!

Next, I went outside and saw:
One yellow sun, Two red birds,
Three green turtles, and my One,
golden-brown dog. I call him Joey,
with a snowy, furry patch.

I headed back to the house—and Oh my! What do I see? A nice round golden-brown pie. It's circle and round just like the sun and moon.

It's round like—my favorite cartoons.

I took a closer look at my grandmother's apple pie.

It's different, but it's a Circle to me. I can certainly say—even though, there is a crust, with a line that is Wavy—just like a bowl of Potatoes with Gravy.

Back to the house, I turn.
I realized: Wow there are so many
shapes and colors to learn. I
wanted to learn to draw all the
shapes that I saw!

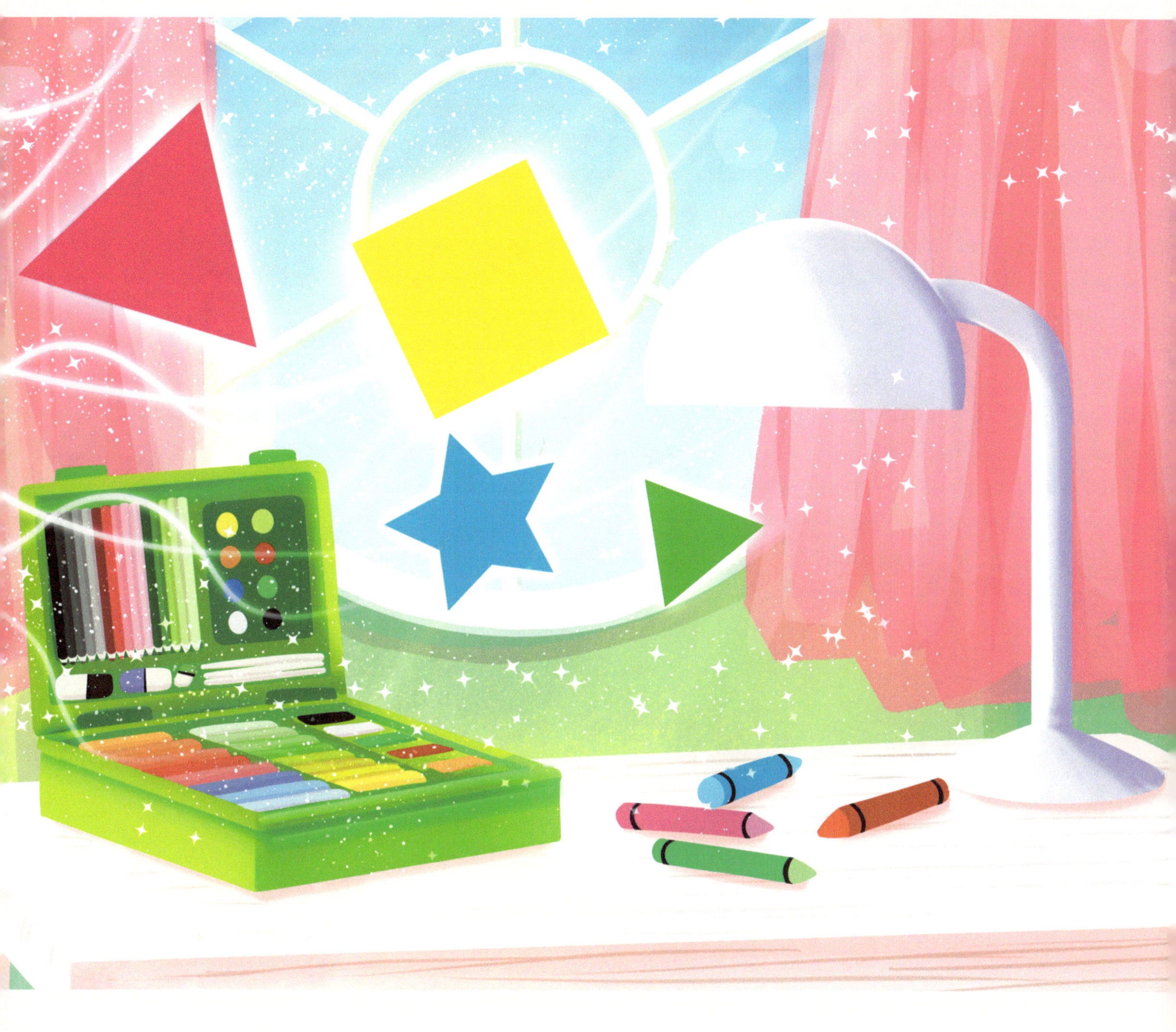

I watched my favorite artist on TV, Ms. Maye Sunshine. She draws shapes, teaches art, and can Doodle, Doodle do!

So, I know what I'll do—I'll try to draw a Circle too.

First, I was excited and told my
mom, "Mommy, I think I can draw!"

Then I asked my Mommy for a
crayon, marker, and paper too. Next,
I would try to Doodle, Doodle, do.

I found a nice spot and placed my drawing on my Green pencil box.

There was a little crack on my Green box—but it was ok—I thought.Surely it would stay together.

I placed my paper on the box and started
to draw, with my Green marker. It is my
favorite color.
I was drawing and drawing and going in a
circle—and then suddenly I heard a "POP"!

My circle got squished and my marker fell
in the crack in my Green pencil box!

Oh, my Doodle, Doodle do!
I was sad because my circle wasn't
round as a pie. It wasn't round as the
beautiful moon, or the sun in the sky.

I told my Mommy and my Dad that I was sad about my drawing. My Mommy asked why. I showed her my circle drawing—she said, "Baby, try again. Keep going and you will win."

My Daddy said, "Sunny, try again, just take your time. But this time—I'll help you Doodle, Doodle, do!"

"Sit at the desk and draw really slow.
Just look at the circle first—and that's
how you'll know," said Daddy.

So, I took a look at a circle, then a look
back and I started to draw really slow,
and then, a little faster.

Before I knew it...my circle was complete!

I added two eyes and a smile, a little hair,
and my circle was there—smiling at me!
I was so happy to see.

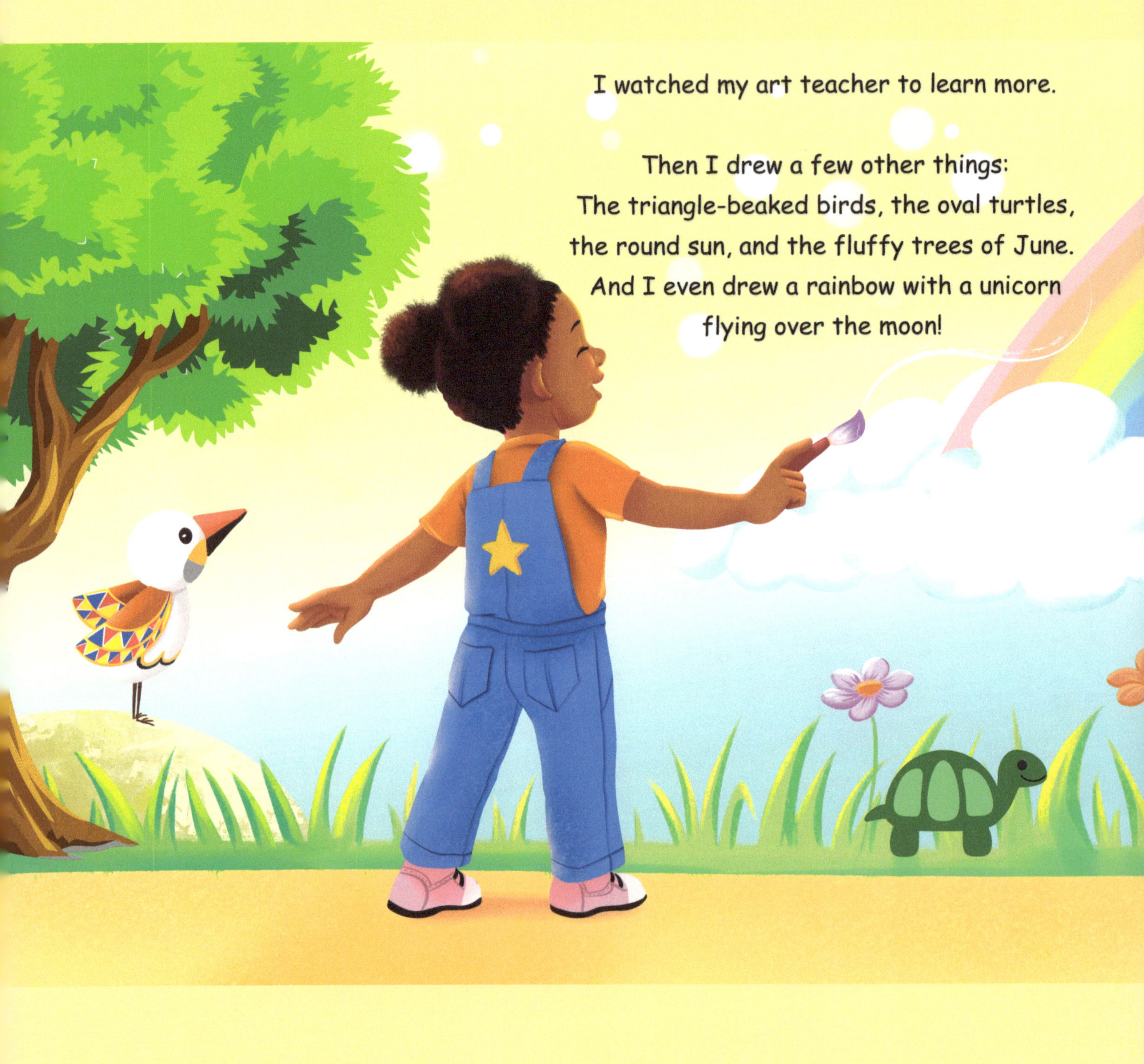

I watched my art teacher to learn more.

Then I drew a few other things:
The triangle-beaked birds, the oval turtles,
the round sun, and the fluffy trees of June.
And I even drew a rainbow with a unicorn
flying over the moon!

Now, I smile and say, "Mommy, look
I can draw, new things."

Then I heard my Daddy say,
"Well, look we have a Little
Artist in the family!"

Yes, she's **the Little Artist!**",
said Mommy.

And all I had to do was take my
time and learn to Doodle,
Doodle do!

Since then, I have drawn lots of things, lots of
Circles, Triangles, Boxes, and Rings.
And the cool thing is they make other things like
birds, animals, and even trains.

Now I can draw, and you can too!

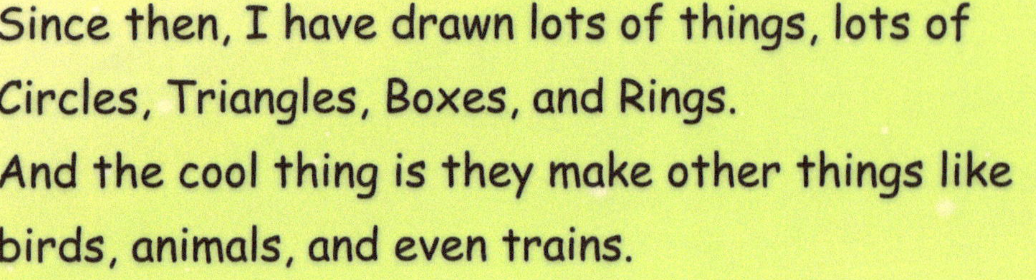

Just take your time next time you—
Doodle, Doodle do.
And it will be true,
that you are a Little Artist too!

See you on Sunny's Next
Big Adventure!

Bonus Page:

One day Sunny had a dream...
She dreamed, that she could draw
anything, and the very thing she'd draw
would come to life!
Like bunnies jumping from a garden,
playing nice—with birdies, and butterflies
and no strife.
"What a dream it would be!" she thought.
And a magical dream it was...

Thank you for reading:
"The Little Artitst,"
a story about the magic of creativity,
learning, family, and never giving up!
Get more creative inspiration and
coloring sheets on our website.

www.LearnMediaPublishing.com

About the Author:

Roshika West is the author and creator of "The Little Artist" book series. West is an accomplished writer and artist, that loves to educate through her works. Her creative journey includes the milestones of attempting to draw a circle at age 5, to learning to draw cartoon comics from the weekly newspapers growing up, to creating realistic oil paintings by the age of 12. West took college-level art at age 17 and she currently has several degrees in media arts. West learned to train others in the arts and has a passion for sharing her experiences through classes, and her creative works including books, training, films and more.

Contact: www.LearnMediaPublishing.com

Acknowledgements:

The author acknowledges and thanks:

-Her creative digital team

-Her family for their support and inspiration

-Finally, thanks to her book readers, family and friends.

Learn Media Today:
Arts and crafts classes from
"The Little Artist":

Online Lessons & Art Kits:
www.learnmediaschool.com

Publisher and Author Booking Contact:

www.learnmediapublishing.com

Author/Artist Website:

www.hellosunshineart.com/about

www.ingramcontent.com/pod-product-compliance
Lightning Source LLC
Chambersburg PA
CBHW042120030726

47599CB00002B/283